Wise Woman Oracle

Reconnect with She Who Knows

Cheyenne Zárate

ROCKPOOL

Acknowledgments

Two cards in the *Wise Woman Oracle* feature quotes: Card 9 from *Women Who Run with the Wolves* by Clarissa Pinkola Estés and Card 25 is by Rebecca Martin (but is strongly associated with Frida Kahlo).

A Rockpool book
PO Box 252
Summer Hill
NSW 2130
Australia

rockpoolpublishing.com

Follow us! **f** 🅞 rockpoolpublishing
Tag your images with #rockpoolpublishing

ISBN: 9781922786050

Published in 2024 by Rockpool Publishing
Copyright text and images © Cheyenne Zárate 2024
Copyright design © Rockpool Publishing 2024

Design and typesetting by Sara Lindberg, Rockpool Publishing
Edited by Lisa Macken

Printed and bound in China
10 9 8 7 6 5 4 3 2 1

Contents

Introduction

Over the past few years I have done a great deal of rewilding within my self with the help of the fiercely independent, untamed, and instinctual archetype of the wild woman. Amid a failing marriage, changing career path, and an all-around identity crisis, her wild medicine was gratefully and graciously received, and I longed to share it with others who were equally in need of her gifts of unapologetic authenticity, freedom, and self-respect. So I did, in the form of my first oracle deck and labor of love: the *Wild Woman Oracle*.

As I write these words, I know within my soul that even though the wild woman still lives within me, I have entered into a different stage of my life and, in so doing, I am connecting with a new feminine archetype in a profound and special way: the wise woman. She is the healer, cunning woman, curandera, priestess, and crone within each and every one of us, who shares her accrued knowledge, wisdom, and experience with others. Although this is the first season in my life when I have consciously connected with the wise woman, it is oddly perhaps one of the archetypes I have most naturally embodied since I was a very young child as my mother labeled me an "old soul." Deep down, I've always loved nurturing the growth of both humans and non-humans and yearned to share what I've learned with others in the hope it may help them in some way.

Within worldwide myth, folklore, and fairy tale, the wise woman is often represented and symbolized by an old crone or grandmotherly figure who has lived a full life, gained immense wisdom and insight through lived experience, and possesses deep knowledge of the natural world that she uses to heal and support those around her. Though she is associated with the waning phase of the moon and the menopause stage of womanhood, the wise woman is not limited by age and she exists within all of us, being awakened and embodied again and again throughout various life stages.

We can find the wise woman at the crossroads between compassion, empathy, and motherly love, and mystery, magic, and the creative and destructive forces of nature. When we enter her time we seek to challenge ourselves and those around us to live up to our highest potential and integrity, and share our knowledge and wisdom with our children and family and also the greater world. All of the earth is an extension of ourselves. As wise women, our sphere of nurturing, teaching, and healing is beyond ourselves, our families, and the human community, guiding, caring for, and inspiring the growth of all life on our beautiful Mother Earth.

The wise woman, or "She Who Knows," is already within you, but it is my deepest hope that the feminine figures within the folkloric, mythological, and contemporary tales featured in the *Wise Woman Oracle* support you in consciously reconnecting with this part of yourself and awakening you to your unique genius, talent, and lived experience that can help you be of greater service and healing in the world.

How to Use the Cards

Each card celebrates an empowering and inspiring feminine figure from myth, folktale, history, or pop culture who embodies the wise woman archetype. This guidebook tells their stories and explains the symbolism inherent in each tale and each card's artwork, then invites you to reflect on the message each card offers.

The *Wise Woman Oracle* is a tool for self-reflection, self-awareness, and personal and spiritual growth that aims to assist you in reconnecting with your inner wise woman. For millennia, the patriarchy has sought to suppress and separate women from unearthing the sacred, ancient knowledge of our ancestors and wise women of old and, in some ways, it has succeeded, but every woman has ancestral wisdom written within her DNA that can never be taken from her. This wisdom and knowing within is what this oracle will help you reawaken to, for you are a granddaughter of the witches – the wise women – they could not burn.

Each card's wise woman possesses unique wisdom to share with you, wisdom that will help you gain insight into the current circumstances that pertain to both your inner and outer worlds. Ponder how the challenges, tests, triumphs, and transformation of each wise woman and her story might apply to your life, then use the wise counsel, guidance, and/or action they offer to reconnect with She Who Knows heal your mind, heart, body, and soul, and become a powerful agent of healing and wisdom within the world in your own unique way.

To use the cards, first shuffle them while you think about what you need, then spread them out face down before choosing a card or cards. Use this guidebook to help you interpret the meaning of each card you are drawn to choose. Outlined below are two helpful methods of divination.

One-card Divination

Select a single card:

- to help you connect with and embody the right energy for the day
- to help you reflect on an issue that needs attention and healing
- to indicate an area of focus for the day
- to indicate a specific affirmation or intention for the day or week.

Three-card Divination

Choosing three cards can give you a more comprehensive insight into a situation. For the three different approaches outlined below, select three cards and lay them face up from left to right.

1. Question, the unseen, and soul assignment

- **Card 1:** represents the question at hand and the energy currently surrounding it.
- **Card 2:** shows what is hidden from view or what you are not seeing.
- **Card 3:** reveals your soul's most significant, urgent assignment and the wise counsel being offered regarding the question or situation.

2. Situation, action, and outcome

- **Card 1:** shows a situation that needs immediate attention or resolution.
- **Card 2:** the action you need to take.
- **Card 3:** the likely outcome if the action is taken.

3. Past, present, and future

- **Card 1, the past:** a valuable lesson that you learned in the recent past.
- **Card 2, the present:** the current energy or situation you find yourself working through.
- **Card 3, the future:** the wisdom and value that you will learn or gain in the future by applying your past learned lesson to your current energy or situation.

Card Messages

1. BURNING TIMES
Integrity

1. BURNING TIMES
⤳⤳ *Integrity* ⤳⤳

*In what area/s of my life is my integrity
being challenged, and how can I stay true to
my core values even when it is difficult?*

As most people were extremely poor in medieval Europe and couldn't afford the medical care of a licensed doctor — incredibly rare to find in Europe in the Middle Ages to begin with — it was commonplace for people to visit a wise woman. They would treat the illnesses and injuries with herbal remedies created from plants, herbs, minerals, and animals from the local landscape. They were trusted and valued members of the community for centuries, but this changed during the witch hunts across Europe and colonial America between the 15th and 18th centuries, when 40,000 to 100,000 women were tortured and executed by the church and ruling elites. Over this span of years, the "women's holocaust," invaluable holistic knowledge and wisdom was lost that we are still trying to recover today.

Symbolism

A wise woman, who is a sacred keeper of invaluable wisdom of the land on which she was raised that was passed down from her mother and mother's mother, is accused of being the devil's consort and practicing witchcraft. As she burns at the stake and gazes into the luminous face of the full moon a look of sheer defiance, courage, and dignity spreads across her face.

Reflection

In the midst of immense hysteria, paranoia, and violence during the witch trials or "burning times" of the Middle Ages, thousands of women rebelliously lived their truth – albeit with as much secrecy as possible due to the very real dangers they faced – and continued to treat and heal those who were in need of their help despite facing possible brutal persecution or death as punishment. You are called to speak and act with integrity, to stay true to your highest values and do what you believe in your heart to be right, like these courageous wise women even if you're facing unjust persecution due to fear or ignorance.

2. ALL HALLOW'S EVE
Purification

2. ALL HALLOW'S EVE
⤜⤜⤜ Purification ⤛⤛⤛

*What endings must I embrace to purify my
soul and life of people, behaviors, beliefs, and
circumstances that no longer serve me?*

The Celts celebrated their new year, Samhain, on the eve of October 31. Translating from Gaelic to "summer's end," Samhain marks the time when the sun dies and rests in peace until its rebirth during the winter solstice. The seeds of the harvest lie dormant and hidden deep within the earth, the leaves on the trees shrivel, the dark nights grow longer, and the earth freezes and falls into a somber slumber. What's more, the witches' new year was when the veil between this world and the otherworld was lifted, allowing humans to reunite with their lost loved ones and ancestors.

Symbolism

As the border between summer and winter, and lightness and darkness, Samhain is a celebration of death. It was a festival of completion to show gratitude for both the labor sown and the bounty reaped throughout the year. Simultaneously, it is a festival that acknowledges the rest, darkness, and silence Mother Earth needs to revitalize herself for next year's harvest. While celebrating death may seem sinister, it is a stark reminder that we live in a never-ending world of cycles. Life, death, and rebirth are seen in the natural world everywhere from the moon, to the animals and the feminine body. Death is a force we must be willing to come face to face with, and also a force we must welcome and revere.

Reflection

The fear that humanity holds about death shows up in many areas, often to our own detriment. We cling tightly to relationships and people who were supposed to walk out of our lives months or years ago. We hold on to jobs or careers that no longer fulfill us and to parts of our self-identity that are false, because the known, although destructive, feels safer than the unknown. You are challenged to embrace endings in many ways. Instead of seeing the ending of relationships, careers, or definitions of self as losses, seek to view them as a process of purification. Think of their removal as the same process the phoenix endures when it bursts into flames and is reborn anew.

3. BEAUTY OF THE CRONE

Ageing

3. BEAUTY OF THE CRONE
Ageing

How can I transform my view and experience of the ageing process so that, with every passing year, I feel more empowered within my body, heart, mind, and soul?

In modern society, women face an immense amount of pressure to remain looking youthful and attractive. We are not allowed to have wrinkles across our faces, let our hair turn gray, or our skin sag. These unrealistic expectations make it increasingly commonplace for women to undergo cosmetic procedures to maintain their youth, and while this is our choice to do so, we must critically question *why* we as women are expected to fight against such a completely natural process such as ageing in the first place.

Symbolism

A woman in her crone stage of life gazes into the starry night sky, which cradles a waning moon and a great horned owl: symbols of her wisdom and inner power. Though she may still have days when she struggles to accept her ageing face and body, a sense of peace and conviction fills her soul as she decides to embrace the natural ageing process, every silvery gray hair that emerges from her head, and look upon each line and wrinkle on her face as a sign of a life fully lived. Her rebellious spirit refuses to let the patriarchy convince her that her value diminishes alongside her youth, and instead walks in the knowing that true invaluable beauty – wisdom, knowledge, kindness, the substance of her character, and the depth of her soul – will continue to grow with time.

Reflection

Long before the world became youth-centric, there was a time in history when the wisdom and sacred knowledge of elderly women were greatly respected and revered, and women were not bombarded with the idea that their value was intrinsically connected with their youth, external beauty, or the ability to bear children. Whether you are personally evolving from maiden to mother or mother to crone, you are called to recognize the unique beauty you possess right now both within and without. Instead of trying to stay eternally youthful, focus on ageing healthily, gracefully, and most importantly gratefully, as ageing is a privilege denied to many.

4. YULE'S EMBRACE
Solitude

4. YULE'S EMBRACE
→⊱ Solitude ⊰←

What are some valuable key insights I have discovered about myself and my deepest truths over the past 12 months?

The winter solstice, or Yule, takes place on December 21. It marks the longest night of the year in winter when the earth is frozen and covered in snow. In the harsh, dark, cold winter we can find it difficult to find any trace of beauty and joy. However, the winter season can be a great teacher and, while perhaps not as vibrant as other seasons, it indeed holds a stoic, quiet beauty. Don't see the darkness as some sort of divine punishment, but as an opportunity to regain balance, insight, and endurance in your life, including the shaping of your character. Winter can be the season of the greatest growth and self-awareness, where you embrace the hermit archetype and refine your sense of self with the wisdom gained throughout the previous seasons.

Symbolism

Spiritually and literally, the winter solstice is a promise of returning light as the days gradually begin to grow longer. While the promise of finding our internal light and of the returning sun in the sky are beautiful things, it is important to not diminish the significance of this sabbat's darkness and make it entirely about awaiting the light of spring. The darkness, the stillness, the solace that winter brings possesses its own mystical boons of introspection, wisdom, and will. We must sit in the most profound depths of the dark season and be open to the treasures it teaches and provides.

Reflection

You are called to slow down, rest, and reassess where you are going and who you are becoming. Like Mother Nature, humans – especially women, as we are cyclical beings who are highly in tune with the changing seasons of the earth and the waxing and waning of the moon – cannot endlessly move at the same quick pace we would in the seasons of light. Do not let this time of darkness and solitude pass you by without using its magical boons. Cherish the lessons and knowledge this year's journey has afforded you and rest your weary, yet wiser, soul.

5. A PLACE OF REFUGE
Refuge

5. A PLACE OF REFUGE
Refuge

What is the dream life, a life that feels like a fulfilling sanctuary, I truly desire to create for myself?

For millennia, women have been expected to center their entire lives around others and what we can do for them. Even the titles and language used to describe women – wife, mother, daughter, sister – demonstrate who we are in relation to others. However, now more than ever women are questioning whether the expectations set for us are truly what *we* desire for our lives, and whether we only want marriage, children, and a white picket fence because those things will make us accepted and valued by society. While there is nothing inherently wrong with a traditional life, to some women that life would feel like a prison and they would prefer a life of solitude living among animal friends.

Symbolism

A woman lives with her two familiars in a country cottage within an enchanted forest full of fairies and gnomes. She yearns for solitude in the heart of the wilderness to live in connection with her self and the cycles of nature. Though she lives an unconventional lifestyle she is happy, content and fulfilled with her choices. Whether she has never been married, left an unhappy marriage, decided to be child free, or is unable to bear children, she is at peace with her individual path and has decided to not let the world dictate what it means to be a fulfilled woman.

Reflection

Women who stray from preconceived notions of what it means to be a happy, whole and fulfilled woman often face criticism and condescension. No matter how much we have achieved and contributed to society in education, careers, and skills, we are still viewed as being incomplete if we are not married with children. You did not incarnate on this earth to live the dream life of someone else; you came here to live your authentic truth. If the white picket fence is what will truly bring you happiness and fulfillment then embrace that life, but if your dream life is traveling and exploring the world, dedicating your life to your career, or being a proud crazy cat lady in a secluded cottage in the woods, embrace *that* life unashamedly.

6. IX CHEL, PROTECTOR OF WOMEN

Empowerment

6. IX CHEL, PROTECTOR
OF WOMEN
>>> *Empowerment* <<<

*Which painful experiences from my life can
I utilize to support, help, and empower others
who have endured similar circumstances?*

Ix Chel is a triple goddess in the Mayan Dresden Codex. As the maiden, she is the goddess of the moon, physical love and fertility. As the mother, she is the goddess of weaving and creativity. As the crone, she is the goddess of medicine, divination, midwifery, the life/death cycle and destruction. Ix Chel had a tumultuous marriage to the sun god Kinich Ahau. Ix Chel's grandfather killed her over his disapproval of the union, and for 13 days dragonflies grieved and sang over her lifeless body until she emerged whole again. Kinich Ahau accused her of having an affair with his brother and threw her from the heavens, so Ix Chel decided to leave him. She turned herself into a jaguar and hid from him in underground caves known as "cenotes." Ever since, Ix Chel has been helping women in need, whether it be nursing them through childbirth or protecting them from abusive relationships.

Symbolism

Ix Chel is worshiped by the Maya of the Yucatán Peninsula, encompassing what is today parts of México, Belize, Guatemala, El Salvador, Honduras, and Nicaragua. Her name means "Lady Rainbow" or "she of the pale face," alluding to the luminous face of the moon. Before the Spanish invaded México and Central America in the 16th century, Maya women who lived in what is now Cancún and its surrounding areas made pilgrimages to the islands of Cozumel and Isla Mujeres to mark their transition from girls to grown women. They gave offerings to Ix Chel and asked for her favor in the hope of receiving the blessings of a long life, happy marriage, and healthy pregnancies.

Reflection

The most disheartening experiences we endure throughout our lifetimes often crack open our hearts to a more profound level of empathy and align us with our soul's purpose. Just as Ix Chel turned her wounds from her abusive marriage into her motivation to protect other women in similar circumstances, you are asked to become an empowerer and protector, through raising awareness, hands-on service, or utilizing your talents and knowledge, to those with whose pain you deeply empathize.

7. SARASWATI, GODDESS OF KNOWLEDGE AND THE ARTS

Self-knowledge

7. SARASWATI, GODDESS OF
KNOWLEDGE AND THE ARTS
◆◆◆ Self-knowledge ◆◆◆

*In what ways have I allowed the illusions of the
world to derail me from my inner truth,
values and purpose, and how can I reconnect
with the essence of my self?*

Saraswati, the Hindu goddess of wisdom, art, music, speech, and learning, is first noted in the Rigveda. Previously significant as a river goddess, Saraswati later became associated with the arts, intelligence, consciousness and creativity. Her name translates from Sanskrit as "she who helps realize the essence of self."

Symbolism

Saraswati is usually depicted as a beautiful woman wearing a white sari with little to no jewelry or bright colors, which symbolizes purity, truth, discrimination, and disinterest in material possessions. Her four arms symbolize aspects of the human personality: mind and sense; intellect and reasoning; imagination and creativity; and self-consciousness and ego. The book she holds symbolizes the Vedas, representing universal, divine knowledge and learning. The garland represents the power of meditation, inner reflection, and spirituality. She is playing the *veena*, representing the arts and sciences and the ability to express knowledge that creates harmony. The swan demonstrates Saraswati's power of discernment, while the peacock symbolizes beauty, the celebration of dance, and the arts. The peacock derives its radiant plumage from the poison of the cobras it eats, representing Saraswati's ability to transmute the poison of the self into beautiful art and wisdom.

Reflection

The Temple of Apollo at Delphi bears the phrase "Know thyself." Saraswati reminds you there is nothing more important in this life than your journey of self-knowledge, as you must understand your inner world's thoughts, feelings, values, and motivations to make healthy decisions, act in alignment with your higher purpose, and alchemize your deepest pain, weaknesses and inner demons into your greatest works of art.

If you have been distracted lately by the illusions and delusions of the material world and have strayed further away from what brings genuine meaning, reconnect with the essence of your true self and move forward to act from a place of integrity and with a refined sense of discernment.

8. BRIGID,
GODDESS OF THE ETERNAL FLAME
Inner Light

8. BRIGID, GODDESS OF
THE ETERNAL FLAME
Inner Light

In which area/s of my life am I struggling to feel hopeful, and how can I renew this sense of hope and ignite the eternal flame within?

The prominent Celtic goddess Brigid is one of the most influential religious figures in Irish history. In Old Irish her name was Bríg, which means power, vigor, virtue, and authority, so Brigid's name is believed to translate to "exalted one." She is the goddess of poetry, healing and smithcraft, and is heavily associated with fire, the sun, creative inspiration, fertility, agriculture, spring, livestock, and childbirth. Brigid is sometimes seen as a triple goddess. Brigid of the Poets is a protector and inspirer of poets, strongly linking her to prophecy. Brigid the Healer is a healer of people and animals, while in Scotland Bride is largely associated with childbirth. As Brigid of the Forge she is the pounding hammer that creates tools of agriculture and warfare to support and protect her people.

Symbolism

Imbolc is celebrated on February 1, marking the beginning of spring, and is a holy day dedicated to Brigid. Although it is now blended and celebrated with the christianized Saint Brigid's Day and Candlemas, Imbolc is undoubtedly a pagan holiday in origin as it celebrates the beginning of the agricultural year when the sheep begin lambing. Historically, the rituals, prayers, and divination enacted on Imbolc were led by women and girls, so they were the main intercessors between Brigid and the family. In Scottish folklore, Bride is said to rule over the light half of the year from Beltane to Samhain, while the dark half of the year is ruled by The Cailleach. The Cailleach's son Angus fell in love with Bride so The Cailleach imprisoned her, which caused cold, dark winter to take over the land. Angus found and freed Bride on Imbolc, loosening winter's grip on the land and giving way to spring.

Reflection

With her connection to Imbolc, light and rebirth, Brigid is the embodiment of spring's first rays of sunshine, which lift our spirits and give us new hope. Like her eternal flame, which burned for over 500 years without producing any ash, Brigid reminds you that even though you may feel as though you have been wandering for days, weeks, or months in darkness, there is an inner, infinite light within you that can never truly be dimmed.

9. THE HANDLESS MAIDEN
Endurance

But it is her soul that is making tears, and they are her protection.

9. THE HANDLESS MAIDEN
Endurance

How is my endurance currently being tested, and how can I tap into my inner knowing and accrued wisdom to help me through this arduous time?

In "The Handless Maiden" folk tale from eastern and middle Europe, an old miller trades his daughter to the devil for great riches. After ordering her not to bathe anymore, the maiden weeps so much that her hands become pure and the devil cannot touch her. Infuriated, he orders the maiden's father to chop off her hands. The girl cries tears over the stumps of her limbs, which purifies them, and the devil is thrown about and loses all claim to her. The handless maiden wanders into the wild woods and stumbles across a royal orchard where a bough bends itself towards her, offering a juicy golden pear. It is in this orchard that she meets her beloved, the king, and ultimately gives birth to his child. While the king is away the devil tries to destroy the queen and her child, but she finds refuge with kindly woodspeople and her hands regrow.

Symbolism

The tale of the handless maiden depicts the journey each woman must embark on to reconnect with the wise woman within. The tears running down the handless maiden's cheeks are her sacred protection from the perils she faces, as tears are a crucial and purifying part of the soul's wise expression.

The cutting of the maiden's hands is symbolic of severing the hands of the ego to regain our wise feminine senses. The pear, a fruit filled with life force, that is offered symbolizes the fact that during even the darkest night of the soul nature feeds and nourishes a woman's soul. By enduring the devil's trickery the maiden becomes wiser and more difficult to fool or corrupt, which is evidenced when her hands regrow.

Reflection

Every woman must undergo a number of initiations that cause her to lose her innocence. When we connect with our deep instinctive knowing and partner this with wisdom gained from lived experience the hands of womanhood return to us, no matter how long they have been cut off. If you are currently being tested, recognize that you possess the feminine wiles to endure whatever the predator in your psyche and outer world throws your way.

10. VESNA'S VICTORY
Bravery

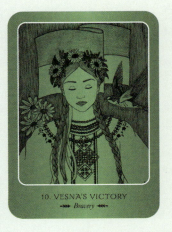

10. VESNA'S VICTORY
◆◆◆ *Bravery* ◆◆◆

*In what way(s) am I currently being called
to be brave and fight in the face of fear?*

In ancient Slavic mythology, Vesna was celebrated as the goddess of spring, rebirth, fertility, and victory in many eastern European countries such as Ukraine, Russia, Croatia, Serbia, North Macedonia and Slovenia. Around the spring equinox, a procession of young women carried an effigy of Vesna out into the fields, singing songs of praise to the goddess. The custom symbolized life's victory over death. The rebirth of nature was also celebrated in other ways, from the making of bellflower wreaths to painting eggs red to symbolize the sun and heat brought by Vesna.

Symbolism

As Vesna's name translates to "spring" she is usually depicted as a young maiden wearing a white dress and a flower crown; she is the personification of spring and renewed hope. Along with a *vinok* (crown) upon her head that features Ukraine's national flower, the sunflower, Vesna wears a traditional Ukrainian embroidered blouse – and Ukraine's national costume – called a *vyshyvanka*, which is used as a talisman to protect the person wearing it. A geometric pattern was weaved by adding red or black threads into the light threads to bestow the wearer with protective power against all harm. The Ukrainian saying "Born in Vyshyvanka" is used to emphasize luck and the ability to survive any situation. More than 6.2 million refugees, predominantly women and children, have been forced to flee Ukraine and leave behind their husbands, brothers and sons to fight in the war. More than 60,000 Ukrainian women serve in the Ukrainian military, while tens of thousands more women serve their country as journalists, teachers, paramedics, politicians, and artists.

Reflection

Just as the ancient Slavs viewed Vesna as an ally and bringer of life in the midst of winter's strife, today the Ukrainian people demonstrate remarkable courage, dignity, and strength of spirit in the face of heartbreaking violence and tyranny. You are called to remember that true bravery comes from standing up for what you believe in, not in the absence of fear but in spite of it. Even though fear is present and victory is uncertain, acting from a place of love, honor, and truth is vital.

11. THE NUTCRACKER AND CLARA'S DANCE

Childlike Wonder

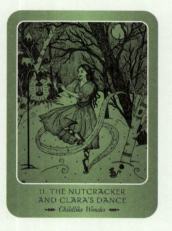

11. THE NUTCRACKER AND CLARA'S DANCE
Childlike Wonder

What activities stimulate my imagination and encourage me to connect with my inner child?

The fairy-tale ballet *The Nutcracker* premiered live for the first time at the Imperial Mariinsky Theatre in St Petersburg, Russia in 1892. Russian composer Pyotr Tchaikovsky, writer of the ballets *Swan Lake* and *Sleeping Beauty*, wrote and composed its ethereal music. As beloved as Clara Stahlbaum and the nutcracker's magical Christmas Eve adventure to the land of sweets after defeating the evil mouse king is today, the ballet did not achieve popularity as a Christmas performance event until almost 100 years later. *The Nutcracker*'s whimsical, notable music, including "Dance of the Sugar Plum Fairy," has been used in several film adaptations of the original story by E.T.A. Hoffmann.

Symbolism

On the eve of Christmas, Clara dances merrily with the nutcracker, given to her as a gift by her eccentric Uncle Drosselmeyer, in the middle of an enchanted forest upon a blanket of freshly fallen snow. Magical light surrounds and begins to engulf them, and it will not be long before the nutcracker comes to life and takes Clara on an unforgettable adventure to the land of sweets. Is this journey they take and the otherworldly beings they meet real, or are they figments of Clara's imagination? We will never know, but it doesn't matter if it's real for Clara.

Reflection

As we grow older we often forget the value of imagination, and we begin to view it as trivial. A true wise woman knows the immeasurable significance of maintaining a child-like wonder about the world within and around us. Our inner child needs imaginative play, a magical process that allows a cardboard box to become a powerful rocket, a bathtub to morph into the deep blue sea, or a wooden nutcracker to transform into a life-size prince. Imagination is integral to self-discovery and personal growth, as it allows us to envision our goals, dreams, and aspirations. Take some time to view the world through a child's eyes to infuse your life with the joy and wonder that imagination brings.

12. RETURNING TO HER SOUL SKIN
Soulful Living

12. RETURNING TO HER SOUL SKIN
Soulful Living

*What places, activities, and ideas light my
soul on fire and make me feel truly alive?*

The selkie is a mystical creature found throughout the mythology of cold countries of the north. Selkie tales are told among the Celts, Scots, indigenous peoples of north-west North America, Siberians, and Icelandic people. In one story a lonely man stole a selkie's skin and forced her to be his wife, promising he would return it after seven summers. They had a child, Ooruk, and the woman's body began to fail. The man didn't return his wife's skin as promised, but Ooruk found it and gave it back to her. Something deep within her soul called her to the sea and she dove into it with her son, and after seven days the luster returned to her body. On the seventh night the seal woman returned Ooruk to his world and disappeared into the icy waters. Ooruk grew to be a mighty drummer, singer, and maker of stories, and he could be seen speaking to a female seal who often came near the shore. Even though many men have tried to hunt her, they have failed time and time again.

Symbolism

Throughout our lives we are domesticated by the beliefs, expectations and desires of our families and cultures until we get to a point where we feel completely alienated from our authentic self. After years of behaving how we think we should we may hear the faint calling of our soul to return somewhere that feels foreign yet familiar. Though this can be a physical place, it is often a more mundane activity such as painting, dancing, reading a book, or letting our hair dry in the sun's heat. The selkie's longing to return to the sea is symbolic of every woman's longing to feel the freedom of living an integral, soulful life or reclaim her wise, wild, feminine nature.

Reflection

You are called to reclaim your untamed feminine nature and live a life that feels good, enriching, and nourishing to your soul, not a life that merely looks good from the outside. If you've been sacrificing your desires and needs in order to keep the peace or avoid being judged for your unconventional lifestyle, it is time to reclaim what is rightfully yours and return to your soul skin.

13. ARADIA,
QUEEN OF WITCHES
Resistance

13. ARADIA, QUEEN
OF WITCHES
➤➤➤ *Resistance* ◄◄◄

*How can I resist the patriarchal dogma that
was forced upon my ancestors, and freely
embody the divine feminine in a way that
is unique and fulfilling to me?*

Aradia is a mysterious and powerful feminine figure who was born in Italy on a full moon on August 13, 1313: a date deeply connected with the divine feminine as there are 13 lunar cycles and women possess 13 menstrual cycles per year. Aradia was born spirit by the goddess of the moon Diana and the god of light and the sun Lucifer. Diana sent her to incarnate on earth to free her poor and oppressed worshippers from slavery at the hands of the Roman Catholic Church and the Italian upper class. It was also claimed that Aradia was a mortal wise woman who was taught witchcraft by her aunt and became known as the "holy witch" or "La Bella Pellegrina" (the Beautiful Pilgrim). She challenged the existing order in 14th-century Italy and taught the oppressed peasants the old religion of Italian witchcraft, or Stregheria, that their ancestors had embraced.

Symbolism

While teaching the religion of the divine feminine, Aradia provided hope to enslaved peasants who were forced to serve the church and the rich, and hide their beliefs and practices in constant fear of persecution. Aradia taught them how to protect themselves through magic and sync with the cycles of nature through ritual observation of the full moon. Regardless of whether she was a mortal, witch, or the true daughter of the gods, Aradia came to earth to help us find our way back to the divine feminine and free us from the shackles of mental, emotional, physical, and spiritual slavery.

Reflection

Aradia said that whenever people had need of anything, if they adored the mighty spirit of Diana they would be freed from slavery. Whether it be through observing the cycles of the moon, celebrating the sabbats within the wheel of the year, studying the pagan beliefs and practices of your ancestors, or fighting for a particular women's issue, you are encouraged to freely and fully embody the divine feminine in your own unique way.

14. THE GREEN WITCH'S APOTHECARY

Guardianship

14. THE GREEN WITCH'S APOTHECARY
⇻⇻⇻ *Guardianship* **⇺⇺⇺**

*How can I use my unique voice, gifts, skills,
and knowledge to protect Mother Earth, and help
create a world that is respectful, reverent,
and safe for all women?*

The knowledge and wisdom of our ancestors, who lived in communion and cooperation with the earth rather than in competition with it, has been suppressed along with those who were punished for possessing it. It is no wonder that so many people are turning towards forms of paganism and witchcraft, particularly green witchcraft. We are starving for knowledge, connection with the earth and its creatures, and the feminine. Because women are inherently connected with the earth, the manner in which nature is treated is reflected in the way women are treated. When Mother Earth and her creatures suffer, the sacred magic of the earth is forgotten and oppressed and so too are women. It is only when the natural world and its kin are respected, honored, and revered that the witches, healers, givers, and protectors of all life will once again be respected, honored, and revered.

Symbolism

On the eve of Litha, the summer solstice, a green witch concocts a magical brew in her apothecary inside a cozy little country cottage. A warm summer breeze rolls through her window and her furry familiar purrs soundly amid plants, herbs, and potions. The witch possesses a deep reverence for the natural world, and a desire to learn about its mysteries and magic. Knowledgeable in the old ways and able to harness the power of nature to cause change in the physical and spiritual worlds, she yearns to protect all living beings of the earth because she knows we protect what we love.

Reflection

Whether or not you identify as a green witch, you are encouraged to connect with your inner witch, healer and wise woman to help heal and protect the earth, your self, and all women. In your unique way, use your voice, gifts, skills, and knowledge to become a guardian of the earth, and teach others about the significance of treating our beloved planet and all life forms with love and respect. Doing so will inevitably create a world that is safer and more reverent towards women.

15. AUGUST EVE
Celebration

15. AUGUST EVE
➤➤➤ *Celebration* ◄◄◄

*What can I do to celebrate myself
and the fruits of my labor?*

On August 1, the Gaelic festival Lughnasadh or August eve is celebrated. It is therefore called the grain harvest, and it is a time for gathering and giving thanks for the abundance that the union of the sun (god) and earth (goddess) bestow in summer. The sabbat marks the halfway point between the summer solstice, Litha, and the autumn equinox, Mabon, and is named after the Celtic sun god Lugh. August is the sacred month of Lugh, who initiated great festivals to commemorate his mother Tailtiu such as honoring the first fruits, circle dancing, athletic contests, and bonfire celebrations.

Symbolism

For many, Lughnasadh can feel bittersweet. Although it is a celebration of joy, it also marks the beginning of the noticeable descent of the sun into the darkness of winter. It is a time of tension, because although light, heat, and life are bountiful, we are simultaneously reminded that the darkness and scarcity of winter are growing nearer. Just as the grain is cut and parts go into freshly baked bread and other parts are stored away for next spring, Lughnasadh holds significance of the sacrifice, transformation, death, and rebirth all of life endures throughout their life cycles. While it is important to prepare for the coming seasons, we can forget to enjoy the wonders of the present season and celebrate the fruits for which we have labored. We may even feel guilty for indulging in pleasure, knowing that another challenging season is ahead.

Reflection

Every good thing must come to an end, but that doesn't make that good thing any less valuable. It makes it even more valuable, as it is a reminder that life is short and we must celebrate the good while it is here. You have come a long way, and the hard work and dedication you have put into your career, health and relationships over the past few months or years has led you to the sweet abundance you are deservedly now reaping. Rest and delight in the joys of being with the people and things you love most without worrying about what tomorrow brings, for tomorrow's woes can wait.

16. MAMA KILLA,
MOON MOTHER OF THE INCA
Moon Magic

16. MAMA KILLA, MOON
MOTHER OF THE INCA
»»» *Moon Magic* «««

How can I use the lunar cycles to enhance my feminine power and create beneficial changes in my life?

Mama Killa, or Mother Moon, is the principal feminine divinity to the Inca, the creators of the largest and most powerful empire in Pre-Columbian America: encompassing parts of modern-day Perú, Ecuador, Bolivia, Argentina, Chile, and Colombia. She is the goddess of the moon, fertility, the Inca calendar, seasons of the harvest, marriage, and the menstrual cycle. Inca women sought the aid and protection of Mama Killa, and many women became her priestesses. The yearly Festival of the Queen coincided with the spring equinox in September, honoring both Mama Killa and La Coya, the queen and legitimate wife of the Sapa Inca emperor. The festival was a time when women displayed their strength and the concerns of all Andean womanhood took center stage.

Symbolism

In Inca mythology the fox fell in love with the moon due to her immaculate beauty. When he rose up into the night sky to steal her, Mama Killa squeezed him up against herself and produced dark patches on the moon, which can still be seen. The Incas believed that during lunar eclipses an animal such as a puma or serpent was attacking Mama Killa. Since they believed that if the animal achieved its aim the world would be left in darkness and humanity would perish, they tried to scare away the animal by throwing weapons, wailing at the top of their lungs, and instructing their dogs to howl at the moon to call her back.

Reflection

Many ancient peoples marked time by the moon to know when to plant, harvest, and store food, and their sacred religious rituals depended greatly on the full moon and waxing and waning lunar cycles. The moon represents the power of woman in its most unique, raw form, as women are yin, cyclical beings like the luminary itself. Although we have largely forgotten how to harness the power of the moon and work with its energy, you are encouraged to connect with the sacred feminine power of the moon and use its different phases to create transformation within your inner spiritual world and the outer material world.

17. MADNESS OF MIS
Insanity

17. MADNESS OF MIS
-*◊*- *Insanity* -*◊*-

*How can I look at my ability to feel deeply as
a superpower and symbol of my humanity
as opposed to a sign of weakness or insanity?*

Mis was the daughter of a powerful ruler named Dáire Dóidgheal, who was slain by a great Irish warrior. When Mis found his corpse she fell into utter madness. Fur and feathers began to grow over her body, and she flew away into the wilderness. A king offered a reward to any man who could capture Mad Mis and re-civilize her into society but any man who tried was torn at by Mis, for she remembered how these fine warrior men had raped and pillaged so many before her. The kind harpist Dubh Ruis was able to gain Mis's trust. He cared for her until her fur and feathers fell away, and eventually Mis asked to return to the world. However, the other warriors felt they had been made a fool of by Dubh Ruis's success with Mis, so they killed him. Heartbroken, Mis journeyed home to the mountains, regrew her fur, feathers and sharp claws and ran with wolves.

Symbolism

Mis realizes that those who are pure of heart are not safe in a man's world. The men who killed countless young men in battle, burned villages of women and children to the ground, and hunted creatures for sport were the same men who hypocritically thought her uncivilized. Those who go mad in society are not crazy; they are, in fact, sane, as they can see the insanity of our dominant civilization and feel deep rage about the violations against all living things. As philosopher Jiddu Krishnamurti once stated, "It is no measure of health to be well adjusted to a profoundly sick society."

Reflection

Many people have historically been scrutinized for not accepting and justifying the cruelty, greed, and abuses of the dominant patriarchal society. Those who live outside the expected parameters of womanhood are deemed crazy or selfish. Although they are labeled as wild, feral women, which at heart they are, they are often the wisest and most civilized as they have souls that are completely pure. If you sometimes feel crazy because you struggle to fit into mainstream society, know that this is a sign that you are awake and tender, and that this corrupt world has not yet worn away your humanity.

18. A MIDNIGHT READ

Curiosity

18. A MIDNIGHT READ
» Curiosity «

What is a topic I would love to explore and learn more about?

Curiosity is an innate human trait characterized by a desire to explore and understand the world. It is the motivation to seek new information, experiences, and knowledge. Curiosity drives us to ask questions, investigate, and engage in activities that stimulate our minds, and at its core it is the desire to understand what we know we don't know. The enduring power of curiosity is a driving force behind learning, innovation, and personal growth, and if not for the insatiable thirst for knowledge inherent in the human condition, many of history's greatest philosophers, inventors, authors, artists, and beyond would have never inspired and progressed humanity forward as they have.

Symbolism

As the clock strikes midnight on a brisk autumn night, a young witch filled with curiosity and a hunger for learning wears her coziest fuzzy socks and sits in her comfy armchair to read a book she has long awaited. More books that she is excited to delve into sit piled up on the floor in front of her magnificent bookshelf, which is filled with classics such as *The Hobbit* and *Grimm's Fairy Tales*, as well as books about the mythology of old and occult secrets and mysteries. While her hot cup of tea brews nearby, her two cats explore their own curiosity: one playing with an intriguing ball of yarn and the other spying on critters and leaves blowing in the wind outside the window.

Reflection

You are encouraged to explore, discover and learn about a topic that has long sparked your curiosity. Read books, watch documentaries, attend a museum exhibit, or take a course to increase your knowledge on your topic and allow yourself to follow wherever your curiosity takes you. You never know what you may learn not only about the world around you, but yourself as well.

19. DÍA DE LOS MUERTOS

Ancestors

19. DÍA DE LOS MUERTOS
Ancestors

How can I uniquely honor and pay homage to my ancestors and those who have gone before me?

Día de los Muertos or the Day of the Dead is a holiday that originated in ancient Mesoamerica – modern-day México and northern Central America – and is also celebrated in South American countries such as Ecuador, Bolivia, Perú, and Brazil and has become popular among the diaspora of Latinos within the U.S. It honors the lives of deceased loved ones and ancestors and is celebrated on November 1 and 2 with a great deal of food, drink, costumes, music, and dance. Día de los Muertos is believed to be a manifestation of syncretism, blending the traditions of the Aztec, Maya and Toltec peoples with Spanish Roman Catholic holidays.

Symbolism

In México the deceased are honored with *ofrendas*, altars built in homes or on graves. If a monarch butterfly is seen at an ofrenda they are thought to be the soul of the deceased visiting their living family. Brightly decorated calaveras de azúcar, or "sugar skulls," are often left on the ofrendas for children who have passed. The skull is used not as a morbid symbol but rather as a whimsical reminder of the cyclicality of life. Skull imagery became a symbol of Día de los Muertos after the death of Mexican artist José Guadalupe Posada in 1913, whose illustrations of La Calavera Catrina – a female skeleton attired with a plumed hat – highlighted death as the inevitable destiny for both the rich and the poor.

Reflection

When we honor our deceased loved ones and ancestors we demonstrate respect and gratitude for their sacrifices and hard work, and the paths they paved for us. By connecting with them we connect with our culture, history, and ourselves, which allows us to better understand our unique place in the world. Whether it be creating an altar, lighting a candle, visiting their graves, making and offering their favorite meal, or researching your family tree and cultural heritage, you are called to build a stronger bond with your ancestors.

20. BABA YAGA,
HARBINGER OF TRANSFORMATION
Adversity

20. BABA YAGA, HARBINGER
OF TRANSFORMATION
»»» *Adversity* «««

*What wisdom and insights might I gain
from the challenges I am facing?*

Baba Yaga is a key figure of Slavic folklore, and is prominent in eastern European countries such as Ukraine, Russia, and Poland, as well as Balkan countries such as Bulgaria. She is often described as a wicked witch who lives in a hut that walks through the forest on magical chicken legs, flies around in a giant mortar and pestle, and feasts on wandering children. Some scholars believe that Baba Yaga's origins associate her with ancient goddesses who embodied the untameable and unpredictable yet wise and maternal nature of the wilderness, Mother Earth, and the feminine spirit.

Symbolism

Baba comes from the word for "grandmother" or "old woman" in many Slavic languages. Many scholars argue over the true meaning of "yaga," however, with some suggesting it could mean "snake," "horror," or "witch." While Baba Yaga does feel reminiscent of the evil witches found in ancient fairy tales she is much more ambiguous, clever, and multidimensional. As an often unexpected harbinger of transformation who possesses the power to either assist or obstruct those she encounters, Baba Yaga brings us uncomfortable truths and revelations and puts us in the path of obstacles that will challenge and refine our characters. Even though Baba Yaga is a sinister and dangerous figure with the goal of eating children and young maidens, they do escape with their lives due to their goodness, integrity, bravery, and resilience.

Reflection

Baba Yaga leads us on an often frightening journey into the dark unknown, so that with courage, strength, and humility we can authentically find our way back to ourselves holding greater wisdom within. If you're enduring a challenging season in your life, Baba Yaga reminds you that adversity is the fire through which great character is forged. Know that you have the ability to successfully navigate the dark woods, seek Baba Yaga's spinning hut on chicken legs, and find your way home to self with newly acquired insight that you were blind to before your journey commenced.

21. SEDNA,
MOTHER OF THE DEEP
Respect

21. SEDNA, MOTHER
OF THE DEEP
➤➤➤ *Respect* ◆

*What boundaries can I put in place to ensure
that my mental, emotional, physical and spiritual
well-being is being honored and respected?*

In Inuit mythology Sedna is the mother of the sea and keeper of the sea animals, and she was worshipped across the arctic regions of Canada, the US (Alaska), Greenland, and Russia. One myth tells that Sedna married an Inuk who promised to abundantly provide for her, but he was a bird in disguise with no hunting skills. Starving, she was rescued by her father, who killed the Inuk, but on the voyage home the birdman's friends caused a huge storm. Fearing he would drown, Anguta threw Sedna into the icy waters but she held on to the kayak, so he cut off her fingers. She sank to the bottom of the ocean, and seals, walruses, whales, and fish were born from each of her severed fingers. She became a half-woman, half-fish goddess of the sea and queen of Adlivun, the Inuit underworld, who held sacred dominion over all the creatures of the vast, deep sea.

Symbolism

Sedna decides how many animals can be slaughtered by the Inuit people. If her animals are disrespected, Sedna punishes the humans with sickness, starvation, and storms. However, if the people righteously provide offerings, the sea creatures return to the hunters. Like many wise woman figures of myth and folklore, Sedna puts human dignity to the test. The true integrity of our souls can only be proven by the honorability of our actions.

Reflection

Like many women, Sedna comprehends betrayal and deceit at the hands of those she deeply loves and trusts. Often the pain and anguish of broken trust catapults us into greater understanding of our true self, including the deep, dark, and cold regions of our psyches that frequently go unexplored, and implores us to stand in our power. If you've been treated cruelly or without the respect you are due, you are reminded that having access to your emotional, mental, physical, and financial resources is a privilege not everyone deserves. Demand respect and set healthy boundaries for your complete well-being.

22. LADY LILITH
Self-sufficiency

22. LADY LILITH
>>> *Self-sufficiency* <<<

*In what ways have I been dimming down my
capabilities to make myself more palatable to others?*

In Jewish mythology, Lilith was the first woman and Adam's wife. God made Adam and Lilith from the same earth, but their relationship grew contentious when Adam ordered Lilith to be subordinate to him. Lilith proclaimed they had been created from the earth and were thus equal, and she refused to take a subordinate position. When Adam attempted to force her to submit, Lilith uttered the secret name of the creator and flew away – thus becoming the first feminist. God created a second wife for Adam from his rib rather than earth so Eve would submit to him as Lilith had not.

Symbolism

In Vedic astrology the feminine path is ruled by the moon and the numeral 2, meaning there are two distinct female paths. These paths correspond with the new and full moon and are represented in Western spirituality as Lilith and Eve. Women who closely identify with the Lilith/new moon path were demonized and coerced into inauthentically following the Eve/full moon path. Lilith women desire to be equals with their romantic partners and have much guidance to give to others. Cultivating their intellect and personality is highly important, as they want to be valued as much more than a sexual object. Incompatible partners are threatened by their capabilities, and feel emasculated by the fact that the Lilith woman may be more competent or knowledgeable. Liliths are unafraid to own their darkness and demand that others also own their darkness. They are truth tellers, and their integrity, vulnerability, and desire for real connection is too much for those who are not ready to do the inner work.

Reflection

Lilith women are frequently deemed to be difficult because they are not easily dominated: they are too inwardly capable. If you're in a relationship where your self-sufficiency, competence, or intelligence are seen as threats to another's ego and you feel you must dim your light to make them feel more needed, then this connection is in misalignment with your core essence and you may have to seek out connections that genuinely celebrate your independence and brilliance.

23. PSYCHE,
GODDESS OF THE SOUL
Transformation

23. PSYCHE, GODDESS
OF THE SOUL
⋙ Transformation ⋘

*What was a time of darkness when I felt separated
from love that I can now see transformed me into
a wiser, more resilient and beautiful soul?*

The tale of Eros and Psyche appears in Metamorphoses, written in the 2nd century CE by Lucius Apuleius. In this tale Aphrodite's son Eros fell in love with Psyche but told her she must not try to see him or ask his name. However, Psyche's jealous sisters convinced her that her husband was a winged serpent beast, so Psyche shone a light on her husband's face while he was sleeping and discovered he was Eros, the god of love and desire. Eros was so betrayed by his wife's mistrust that he flew away. When Psyche asked Aphrodite to reunite her with Eros, Aphrodite gave her four impossible tasks to complete before she would reunite the lovers. As Psyche descended to the underworld to collect some of Persephone's beauty from a box, the fourth task, she found only death and died. Eros kissed her, awakening her from her eternal slumber. Zeus gave Psyche ambrosia, the drink of immortality, and she transformed into the goddess of the soul.

Symbolism

Psyche is often represented by a butterfly-winged woman, as both the ancient Greeks and Romans represented the souls of deceased loved ones as butterflies. The myth of Eros and Psyche is one of the greatest love stories in classical mythology, and is also widely interpreted as an allegory for the journey of the soul to unite with divine love. Psyche's separation from Eros signifies the journey the soul must take into the unconscious to retrieve abandoned parts of the self and learn to deny the earthly attachments that deter us from our souls' true purpose, before returning to love and wholeness.

Reflection

While we would like to believe we desire a life that is entirely without trials or tribulations, we would never transform and build greater character and tenacity without them. Just like the butterfly undergoing metamorphosis must struggle to escape her cocoon to build strength in her wings to embark on her new journey, so too must our souls undergo great challenges to become resilient, discerning, and wise.

24. OSTARA EVE
Renewal

24. OSTARA EVE
Renewal

What ideas, goals, and intentions do I want to plant and water at this time with renewed hope and excitement?

The history of Ostara, the spring equinox, can be traced back to pre-Christian times, when ancient Germanic and Celtic peoples celebrated the arrival of spring with festivals dedicated to their goddesses of fertility and rebirth. The festival was often associated with Eostre, who was worshipped as the bringer of light. Ostara celebrates rebirth, fertility, growth, and renewal, and is celebrated with activities such as decorating eggs, planting seeds, holding feasts with traditional fresh spring foods, and gathering flowers and greenery to decorate homes and altars. This sabbat marks a turning point of change within the cycles of Mother Earth and initiates the beginning of the agricultural season, when farmers plant seeds so they can reap an abundant harvest and animals give birth to their young.

Symbolism

A solitary witch meditates peacefully deep within the woods on Ostara eve, accompanied by many magical woodland younglings that recently took their first breaths. From her heart chakra, life force emerges as she settles into a deep space of serenity and fearlessly opens up her heart to rebirths, growth, and unknown experiences. The spring equinox marks the astrological new year in the cardinal fire sign of Aries, which is associated with new beginnings, passion, creativity, and courage. Aries is life force and the will to exist, and the first zodiacal archetype: the first step made by consciousness into the outside world.

Reflection

As Ostara honors the return of light, the growth of new life, and the renewal of hope, this card signals this is an auspicious time to metaphorically plant and water seeds in the form of ideas, goals, and intentions you wish to harvest over the following months and year. Open yourself up to the fresh opportunities, beginnings, and learning that are coming your way, and embody the courage, passion, and enthusiasm necessary to bring them into fruition.

25. LA FRIDA
Self-identity

I used to think I was the strangest person in the world but then I thought there are so many people in the world, there must be someone just like me who feels bizarre and flawed in the same ways I do.

25. LA FRIDA
⟫⟫ *Self-identity* ⟪⟪

*What strange and unique qualities, values, passions,
and interests make up my personal sense of identity?*

Frida Kahlo is one of the most important painters of the 20th century. She was born on July 6, 1907 in México to a German Jewish father and Mexican mother of mixed Spanish and indigenous blood. Throughout most of her short life Frida suffered from the chronic pain of polio, which caused one leg to be shorter and thinner than the other, and from a bus accident in which she was impaled by an iron handrail through her pelvis. While confined to her bed in solitude Frida began painting what she knew best: herself. Through her art she openly and bravely grappled with womanhood, heartache, sexuality, feminism, machismo, race, and social class and how they uniquely intertwined to form her self-identity.

Symbolism

Frida was a multifaceted woman who spoke and painted her bizarre and radical truth with boldness and brutal honesty. Her artwork and existence as an openly feminist, bisexual woman of color were acts of rebellion, and she embraced her unconventional beauty and femininity by proudly wearing and painting herself with her iconic unibrow and traditional indigenous Mexican clothing. Frida was part of the Mexicanidad movement, which sought to dismantle colonial ideals and promote a sense of Mexican identity and pride. She was a champion of social justice and the marginalized.

Reflection

Frida unapologetically embraced aspects of herself that had been subjugated, judged, and disrespected throughout history – her unorthodox form of womanhood, mixed ancestry, disability, and unique appearance – and claimed them as key definers of her self-identity. Her legacy proclaims that we are beautiful and valuable not in spite of what the dominant culture may deem as bizarre, but because of it. Just as the personal sides Frida infused into her artwork with all their imperfections, you are called to a higher level of authenticity: to proudly, lovingly, and powerfully claim a self-identity that is built on the foundation of everything that makes you unique, remarkable, and wonderfully flawed.

26. CINDERELLA,
HAVE COURAGE AND BE KIND
Graciousness

26. CINDERELLA, HAVE
COURAGE AND BE KIND
➤➤➤ *Graciousness* ➤➤➤

*When and how have I seen genuine goodness
rewarded in my life, the lives of those around
me, and the greater world at large?*

The earliest rendition of the Cinderella folk tale is the story of Rhodopis, which was recounted between 7 BCE and 23 CE. The most widely known version was published by Charles Perrault in 1697, while a darker version was published by the Brothers Grimm in 1812. Each Cinderella tale usually features a young woman living in challenging circumstances, when all of a sudden, and often with the help of magical beings and animal friends, her fortune changes as she attracts the attention of a nobleman. The nobleman must find out her identity, and when found Cinderella becomes the spouse of royalty. Her evil family members get their just payback for their cruelty.

Symbolism

To diminish Cinderella to nothing more than a weak woman waiting to be rescued would be an injustice. Her story is about the strength, resourcefulness, and hope needed to remain kind and compassionate in the face of immense trials. Cinderella is a dreamer, although her dream is not to marry a prince and live happily ever after but to be happy and free. She is well aware of the abuse she faces, and instead of overtly fighting against it she builds a reservoir of strength and maintains self-control. Her friendships with her animal companions are built on kindness and reciprocity. The hope in her heart that manifests as her fairy godmother, symbolic of her inner wise woman, aids her when she feels that her stepfamily has crushed her spirit entirely.

Reflection

Cinderella is a rags to riches story about a woman who steals the heart of the royal prince and becomes queen, not because of how beautiful she is but because of how gracious and queenly she is on the inside. If you feel discouraged or defeated in the pursuit of your dream, know that your hard work, diligence, humility, and kindness have not gone unnoticed. Divine justice exists, and there are forces both mundane and supernatural that will come to your aid and help make your dreams come true if you are noble and kind-hearted.

27. AJÁ,
FIRST HERBAL HEALER
Reciprocity

27. AJÁ, FIRST HERBAL HEALER
»»» *Reciprocity* **«««**

*What can I give to others that makes me feel
more abundant and grateful by doing so?*

Ajá is an Orisha, a goddess of the Yoruba of West Africa and several religions of the African diaspora such as Cuban, Dominican and Puerto Rican Santería and Brazilian Candomblé. She rules over the forest, woodland animals, and herbal healers and is also known as the "wild wind," as she is the soul of the woodland and creatures within it. Ajá would search for plants with medicinal properties and mix them with herbs and roots to create natural cures for the sick. If someone is carried away by Ajá and then returns, they become a powerful *babalawo* (witch doctor). Ajá peacefully reveals herself to humans who seek her wisdom to teach, guide, and heal them.

Symbolism

Rather than scaring or harming humans to keep them away from natural sites, Ajá generously extends her realms to humans so we may know the significance and sacredness of the forest and its life forms. Consumerism and greed have caused humanity to commit grave acts of injustice against the earth and its creatures. From fighting wars over natural resources, to environmental policies that cause immense harm to the already disenfranchised, we as a collective have lost our reciprocal and symbiotic relationship with the earth. Believing that the earth's abundance provides everything needed to sustain life is a revolutionary idea, as fulfilled and grateful people who live by the law of reciprocity do not take more than what is needed and respectfully use what is freely given to us by Mother Earth.

Reflection

Ajá represents the generosity and healing abilities the earth possesses for our bodies, minds, hearts, and spirits. In a consumerist society that thrives on telling us we never have enough, believing in our inherent value and that every life form is generously sustaining life is a radical proposition. If your soul has been in a state of scarcity you are encouraged to observe the abundance of the natural world around you and, like Ajá, share what has been given to you. Know that you are enough, and that when you give freely with an open heart you help heal the world of its many ills.

28. ATHENA,
GRAY-EYED GODDESS
Reason

28. ATHENA,
GRAY-EYED GODDESS
-»»» *Reason* «««-

*In what situation am I being challenged
and called to respond with my head over my
heart to reap the best possible results?*

Athena is the Greek goddess of wisdom, courage, warfare strategy, handcrafts, and heroic endeavors and is the patroness of various cities. Since the Renaissance she has become an international symbol of wisdom, the arts, and classical learning, and Western artists and allegorists have often used her as a symbol of freedom and democracy. Athena sprung straight from the head of the king of the gods, Zeus, as a fully grown, armored woman. She was the wisest of all the gods and Zeus's most trusted and favorite child, and was also a great adviser, patron, and ally of heroic men such as Odysseus and Achilles.

Symbolism

Athena's most common epithet is "bright-eyed" or "gray-eyed." As the owl is one of Athena's main symbols, the latter speaks to her keen perceptiveness, wisdom, and ability to discern what is truthful in the midst of darkness and deception. Athena is often depicted as a stately warrior goddess wearing gold armor, with the visor of her helmet pushed back to reveal her beauty, and carrying a shield or a spear. She gave Bellerophon a bridle to tame the winged horse Pegasus, and is credited with teaching humans how to build the plow, rake, ox yoke, and chariot. The martial and domestic skills associated her pertain to activities that require purposeful thinking, planning, and execution. Athena values rational thinking, will, and intellect over instinct and nature.

Reflection

Athena reminds you that there are times when it is wise to react from a place of rationality, stoicism, and logic. If you are in the midst of an emotionally charged situation where your gut reaction may make the matter worse or reap negative consequences, take a step back and connect with your inner sage, who is armored in profound wisdom, is an intelligent thinker, is ruled by their head rather than their heart when it is necessary, and who knows that silence is sometimes the most powerful response of all.

29. HECATE,
TORCHBEARER OF TRUTH
Illumination

**29. HECATE, TORCHBEARER
OF TRUTH**
⤛⤜⤛ *Illumination* ⤛⤜⤛

*What truth is ready to finally be illuminated
that will ultimately catapult me into a higher
level of consciousness and wisdom?*

The elusive goddess Hecate has gone through various transformations that encompass every aspect of human life and death. She is a goddess of magic and witchcraft, and is renowned for her knowledge of the healing powers of plants. She is often depicted with three faces and bodies, which reflect her role as a goddess of the crossroads and liminal spaces and the passages between the realms of life and death, connecting her to the underworld, ghosts, the moon, and various animals – especially black dogs, snakes, cats, frogs, and creatures of the night. Hecate also rules over female initiation, including marriage and childbirth, and her favorite people are midwives, witches, healers, herbalists, and dog lovers. She has immense compassion and devotion to truth.

Symbolism

When Persephone was abducted by Hades, it was Hecate who guided her from the underworld with her fiery torch in hand to illuminate the way. This signified that Persephone now possessed the consciousness and wisdom acquired from her journey, a journey initiated and aided by Hecate in her wise woman aspect. Persephone's abduction and return not only mirrors every human's descent into seasons of strife, difficulty, and tribulation, but also demonstrates the important role that women, and particularly older women, have in supporting, witnessing, and guiding other, more inexperienced and naive women. Hecate is the wise companion within every woman who has been to hell and back and emerged with greater depth and wisdom, and she is also the wise counselor all women should strive to be for one another.

Reflection

Hecate urges you to descend into the underworld and seek the truth regardless of how ugly it may be. Even though it may be painful to face, illuminating that which is hiding in the dark will allow you to make wiser choices and take more empowering actions. If this truth is exceptionally distressing to confront and you feel lost in navigating it on your own, seek sage counsel from a respected elder or soul who embodies the wise, silver-haired crone, regardless of age.

30. PRACTICAL MAGIC
Witch Wound

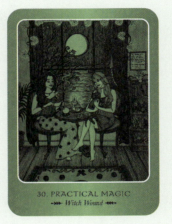

30. PRACTICAL MAGIC
»»* *Witch Wound* *«««

*Which parts of myself have I long suppressed
and feared that I am now ready to begin
openly embracing and expressing?*

The 1998 witchy cult classic *Practical Magic* explores the lives of the Owens sisters and their whimsical aunts. Within the story the Owens women's ancestor Maria Owens escaped an attempted execution for witchcraft. When the father of Maria's child never returned, she cast a spell to prevent herself from ever falling in love again. That evolved into a curse that claimed the life of any man an Owens woman loved. For over three centuries the Owens women were met with suspicion and persecution by the townsfolk. After Sally Owens' husband died due to the curse she vowed that her daughters would never practice magic, but when she had to use magic to save her beloved sister Gillian she learned to embrace her true self and claim her power. Through this reclamation of authenticity she found her true love and taught her daughters magic, and the women were finally accepted as witches. Her witch wound was healed.

Symbolism

Due to our long history of facing persecution and violence at the hands of the patriarchy, imperialism, and religious tyranny so many women are afraid of embracing and expressing their true selves. The fear of persecution and being found out lives deep within our DNA. The witch wound is an inherited psychological and spiritual wound carried by many women who have been taught to fear their feminine power. It can stem from past lives, the culture we were born into, childhood, subconscious programming, and institutions such as the education system and church. It often manifests as a fear of expressing ourselves, of being truly seen and heard.

Reflection

While we do live in a world where bigotry and ignorance still exist, many of us no longer face the threat of execution: even though our survival instinct may tell us differently. Know that you are safe; it is okay for you to step into your feminine power and express your truth and to hold beliefs and values that are different from mainstream culture and religion. Embrace your magic, as being normal is not necessarily a virtue but a lack of courage.

31. AKHILANDA,
SHE WHO IS NEVER NOT BROKEN
Reinvention

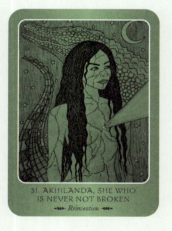

31. AKHILANDA, SHE WHO
IS NEVER NOT BROKEN
⇢ *Reinvention* ⇠

How can I vulnerably and compassionately embrace my brokenness so I can reinvent a self that is stronger, wiser, and more beautiful within?

The mysterious Hindu goddess whose name translates to "she who is never not broken" reminds us that within the darkest times we are at our most powerful, as there is nothing left to lose. Akhilanda is the essence of the phoenix, encouraging us to let our ego's idea of who we think we are go up in flames so we can recreate a more authentic version of ourselves. Depicted with her body divided in many floating pieces, Akhilanda teaches us to embrace imperfection and change. If we never experienced heartbreak or disaster we would never have the opportunity to evolve. Akhilanda tells us that the liminal space where we don't know how to move forward is an empowering place. There we get to consciously choose how we want to put ourselves back together.

Symbolism

Akhilanda's mode of transportation, a ferocious crocodile, represents our primal instincts. Instead of suppressing her fear, Akhilanda rides it down the river. As the crocodile spins its prey in its jaws, disorienting it so it drowns, Akhilanda spins us in her jaws until we are so confused about who we are that we can only allow our ego's identity and attachments to dissolve. The Japanese art form of *kintsugi*, in which broken pottery is fixed by infusing gold into the cracks, is based on the idea that in embracing flaws we can create a stronger, more beautiful piece of art. We are always able to alchemize our pain and insecurities into greater wisdom and beauty. When we release our assumptions and illusions we can bring our darkness into the light and embody the truth that we can never truly be broken because we always are.

Reflection

Akhilanda urges you to discard ideologies, habits, and versions of your self that are disingenuous, stagnant, and obsolete. While your ego may be panicking and holding on tightly to what you have believed for so long about who you are and the world around you, recognize the infinite potential that is available to you to reinvent your self. Allow yourself to fall apart and put yourself back together again with the wisdom and self-awareness you have gained from navigating through the darkness.

32. STEVIE NICKS, THE LEGEND

Dedication

Don't be a lady. Be a legend.

32. STEVIE NICKS, THE LEGEND
->>> *Dedication* <<<-

*What is the personal mission of my life, my
contribution to humanity, and how can I embody
it with greater dedication and authenticity?*

Stephanie "Stevie" Nicks was born in Phoenix, Arizona in 1948, and her passion for music was founded at a young age. Her mother was extremely supportive of her daughter but also very strict, and she told Stevie she should never depend on a man to bolster her. When Stevie wrote her first song at the age of 16 she knew that writing songs and singing them to people was the only thing she could ever do. She worked as a waitress and house cleaner to support herself and faced a great deal of rejection and hardship. In 1975 she joined Fleetwood Mac, and the band quickly achieved worldwide success largely thanks to Nicks's hauntingly beautiful, witchy anthem "Rhiannon." Stevie has been dubbed the reigning queen of rock and roll, and she was twice inducted into the Rock and Roll Hall of Fame with Fleetwood Mac and for her solo work.

Symbolism

Stevie Nicks's work ethic and dedication to her craft as an artist is profound, and it's awe-inspiring that she reached such levels of artistic success without compromising her authenticity. She embraced her feminine power within her lyrics and her bohemian, witchy, ethereal style in an incredibly misogynistic industry. She made a feminist statement in not having children but instead dedicating her life to her world mission of healing people's hearts and making people happy through her music. She claimed herself to be a totally free and independent woman.

Reflection

Talent is not necessarily an accurate indicator or predictor of success, as legends are not born; they are made. Just as the white witch Stevie Nicks was relentlessly dedicated to her mission to heal people through the power of music, you are called to recognize your individual mission on earth and fight for it with impassioned dedication, perseverance, personal power, and authenticity.

33. MABON'S BLESSINGS

Gratitude

33. MABON'S BLESSINGS
⋙ *Gratitude* ⋘

What blessings have manifested into my life that at some point in the past were mere distant hopes and dreams?

Mabon, the autumn equinox and the last sabbat in the pagan wheel of the year, marks the end of summer. As the second of three harvest festivals it is historically associated with giving thanks, as this is the time of year that farmers take stock of their crops and gather the bounty of the harvest they have so carefully grown and tended to during the spring and summer seasons. It is the time of reaping what you sow, and for many ancient peoples the abundance of food or lack thereof harvested around the autumn equinox determined how much food security they would have during the frigid winter months ahead.

Symbolism

In modern culture we are expected to be in an eternal state of blooming and growth, or spring and summer. However, as a part of nature we must also go through seasons of release, rest, and giving thanks. While there is nothing wrong with achieving and wanting more for ourselves, it is important to also relish and feel gratitude for where we are and how far we have come. How easy it is to forget that who we are today and what we have accomplished were yesterday's hopes and dreams. Feeling gratitude for what is calls into our lives more to be grateful for in the future.

Reflection

Even if you are not in the midst of celebrating the literal sabbat of Mabon you are encouraged to take stock of the bounty you are reaping due to your focused intentions, passion, hard work, acumen, and determination. Whether you started your dream business, went back to school to study a subject that has always fascinated you, developed greater focus by meditating daily for 10 minutes, or learned a new language or skill over the past year, thank the divine, your guides, your ancestors, and yourself for the many big and small blessings that surround you.

34. A MOTHER'S LOVE
Nurturing

34. A MOTHER'S LOVE
◆◆◆ *Nurturing* ◆◆◆

In what ways am I embodying the mother archetype, and which parts of myself are in need of extra love, nurturing, and attention?

Historically, at the winter solstice of Yule the goddess, representing the earth, was believed to transition from her crone aspect into her mother aspect. She gave birth to the god, representing the sun, and remained still and silent as she rested from her labor. The mother is one of the primary archetypes within the collective unconscious of humanity: it seems to contain all else, and some of the earliest known artefacts of human prehistory are representations of female fertility and motherhood. The mother possesses inherent light and shadow qualities that have been manifested in many ways; however, in the light form the great mother is a natural caregiver who nurtures others and fosters growth. Being of service to others brings her genuine joy.

Symbolism

On Christmas Eve, a mother and her daughter read the classic poem "The Night Before Christmas," surrounded by the comforts of the Yuletide season. While this woman, having birthed a child into the world, is a mother in the traditional sense, this is not the only way the mother archetype can be manifested. From providing a safe and loving home to our fur babies to advocating for social justice causes, educating and passing down knowledge to younger generations and caring for loved ones who are sick or elderly, women tend to be natural nurturers and instinctually give of ourselves in a variety of ways. We can sometimes extend *too* much of ourselves, to the point we enter the realm of the dark mother, where we neglect ourselves and prioritize everyone else's needs above our own.

Reflection

You are encouraged to become aware of the ways in which you embody the mother archetype, and examine who and what you are nurturing and providing mental, emotional, physical, and spiritual nourishment to. Ask yourself if that which you are mothering is truly a worthy receiver of your nurturing attention or if redirection is needed. If you have been putting your needs and well-being on the backburner, it's time to mother yourself and extend the same love and nurturing to yourself that you offer to others.

35. FRIGG, ALL-MOTHER
Devotion

35. FRIGG, ALL-MOTHER
⋙ *Devotion* **⋘**

*How can I deepen my devotion to the beloved creations
that bring me inner fulfillment and purpose?*

Frigg is the all-mother, the highest of the Norse goddesses, and wife to the all-father Odin. She is strongly associated with motherhood, marriage, fertility, and prophecy. Within the Prose Edda, an Old Norse textbook written in Iceland during the early 13th century by Snorri Sturluson, it is said that once Frigg prophesied through perilous dreams that her son Baldur would meet his doom she approached every living and non-living entity and obtained oaths from them to never harm Baldur. However, she unknowingly revealed to the trickster god Loki that she had not demanded the oath from the humble sprig of mistletoe, which ultimately led to Baldur's death when Loki crafted a spear of mistletoe that struck Baldur in the heart. Overwhelmed with sorrow, Frigg cried such bountiful tears that the mistletoe vowed it would only ever bear white berries formed from Frigg's tears.

Symbolism

Frigg is a seeress or "völva," a Viking practitioner of the Norse magic *seidr*, which involved discerning the course of fate and working within its structure to bring about change. Her weaving ability is an allusion to this role. The spindle, the runes she haphazardly casts, and the keys that hang from her belt indicate her ability to unlock all doors and her oracular and mediumship powers. The stork, a bird associated with motherhood, birth, intuition, and the protection of women and children, bears a sprig of mistletoe in its beak, which symbolizes Frigg's legacy of unrelenting love and devotion and the reverence all creation possesses for her. Women who are giving birth still invoke the blessing of Frigg with a white candle that last burned during the winter solstice, as this is believed to be a charm that ensures a safe and healthy delivery.

Reflection

Frigg calls you to pour your devotion into all that you birth into this world and protect it at all costs. Whether your labor of love is a career you're passionate about, an art form that allows you to express your soul, an invention that moves humanity forward, or children who will make the world a better place, your creations and what you love most are what make life worth living.

36. THE CAILLEACH,
QUEEN OF WINTER
Dark Feminine

36. THE CAILLEACH,
QUEEN OF WINTER
Dark Feminine

In what ways have I repressed my fierce, dark, feminine power in fear that it would make me unlikeable, intimidating, or too much?

The Cailleach is one of the great Celtic ancestors of the Gaelic-speaking world, particularly dwelling in Scotland, Ireland, and the Isle of Man. She is the divine hag of Celtic mythology, and is known as the "Queen of Winter" as she is the goddess of winds, storms, wilderness, and the winter. She often appears as an old crone wearing a black cloak and possessing wild hair. Her face is wrinkled and weathered, and has either blue or extremely pale skin. The Cailleach is a force of nature and the patron of animals, a wise woman who holds age-old wisdom or a seer of that which lies beyond the veil. She is the personification of the fiercest aspects of Mother Nature. In Scottish myth The Cailleach appeared in the sky riding a giant wolf on Samhain, and she would tap her magical staff on the ground and cause it to freeze, thus ushering in winter.

Symbolism

The Cailleach was neither entirely good nor evil. She was a natural and wild destructive force, yet she also created many hills and mountains in Scotland and Ireland, and cared deeply for wild and domestic animals during the difficult winter months. She was the patron of wolves emboldened by winter hunger, and she also served as a deer herder. Hunters have mutual respect for The Cailleach as she ensures a healthy population of deer to provide food and pelts. In return, the hunters must obey her instructions regarding which deer to cull and when, controlling the balance between humans and nature, or face dire consequences.

Reflection

As the personification of winter, storms, and the life/death/life cycle, The Cailleach encourages you to stand in your dark and transformative feminine power. Though women are often expected to always embody the soft, delicate form of femininity and are gaslit into believing that not adhering to this one-dimensional standard makes us too intimidating, The Cailleach urges you to step into your fearsomeness and remember that true femininity is not always flowery and warm. It is sometimes cut-throat and catastrophic, and it is this destructiveness of existing structures and beliefs that makes way for new growth, regeneration, and possibilities.

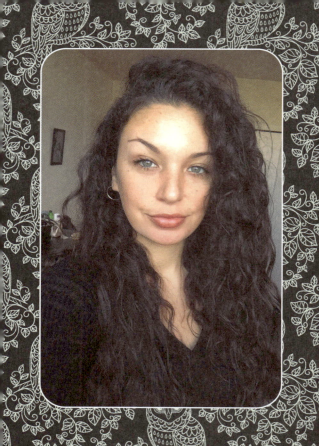

About the Author and Artist

Cheyenne Zárate is an artist, writer, educator, animal and nature lover, and self-proclaimed crazy cat lady and cat mom of four: Carlos, Lily, Ix Chel, and Freyja. She is of mixed Chilean, Ukrainian and Scottish ancestry, which has fostered a unique love and respect for myth and folklore from cultures all around the world that can be seen within her art.

At the age of four, Cheyenne discovered her passion for drawing and would spend hours each and every day bringing the images floating around in her imagination to life on paper. After graduating from the University of Toronto with a Bachelor of Arts in English and Spanish, and York University with a Bachelor of Education, she became an elementary school teacher. Although in many ways she loved teaching and mentoring children, after a few years of teaching in the classroom full time she went through a spiritual awakening and embarked on a journey of self-discovery that ultimately led to her soul calling her onto a different path: a path that blended her love for teaching and education with her inner child's passion for art, nature, mythology, and magic.

Cheyenne believes that art has the power to change and transform the world. Through her artwork and written retellings and analyses about empowering feminine figures from ancient mythology, folklore, and the modern world, she aims to inspire and help all people, especially women, to reconnect with their innate wild, wise, feminine natures in order to live in alignment with their authentic truth and connect with the cycles of Mother Earth.

etsy.com/ca/shop/ArtbyCheyenneZarate

instagram.com/che.zarate

facebook.com/cheyennezarate